BUILDING CONFIDENCE THROUGH SELF-LOVE

A GUIDE TO ACHIEVING SELF-ACCEPTANCE

DR. JAGADEESH PILLAI

Made with ♥ on the Notion Press Platform
www.notionpress.com

|| *Dedicated to all wisdom seekers around the World* ||

ॐ

Contents

Contents

PRAYER

Saraswati Namasthubhyam Varade Kamarupini Vidyarambham Karishyami Siddhir Bavathume Sadh

Greetings to Devi Saraswati, the benevolent granter of blessings and fulfiller of desires. O Devi, as I embark on my studies, I humbly ask that you grant me the wisdom to comprehend correctly.

ॐ

About the Author

Dr. Jagadeesh Pillai is a renowned Guinness World Record holder, writer, and researcher hailing from Varanasi, also known as the abode of Lord Shiva. With a Ph.D. in Vedic Science and a range of creative ideas and achievements, he is a true polymath. He is the author of more than 100 books including Research Publications. Although his roots can be traced back to Kerala, the people of Varanasi hold him in high regard and affectionately consider him one of their own.

In 1998, Dr. Pillai was offered a job at Banaras Hindu University, but he left the position after only two months to pursue greater goals in life. He believed that in order to study Indian scriptures and engage in other creative endeavours, he needed to retire from the daily grind of working solely for money at a young age.

He started an export business from scratch, using the knowledge he had gained from a previous job in the industry. His intelligence and unique approach to business led to great success in a short period of time, earning him more in just a decade and a half than he would have in a lifetime working in a government job. Upon the passing of Dr. APJ Abdul Kalam, Dr. Pillai decided to leave the business and dedicate himself to reading, studying, researching, and experimenting.

During his tenure in the export business, Dr. Pillai traveled to over 16 countries, gaining valuable insight and experiencing the world and life in detail.

Dr. Pillai has achieved four Guinness World Records in the following subjects:

"Script to Screen" - In this record, Dr. Pillai produced and directed an animation film within the shortest time possible, breaking the previous record set by Canadians. He has also received numerous national and international awards and recognitions for this achievement.

Longest Line of Postcards - For this record, Dr. Pillai created a line of 16,300 postcards on the occasion of the 163rd anniversary of Indian Postal Day. The event also included a questionnaire about the Indian flag.

Largest Poster Awareness Campaign - Dr. Pillai designed an awareness campaign on the subject of "Beti Bachao - Beti Padhao" (Save the Girl Child - Educate the Girl Child) to achieve this record.

Largest Envelope - In tribute to the Indian Prime Minister's "Make in India" initiative, Dr. Pillai created a 4000 square meter envelope using waste paper to achieve this record.

Attempted - **70000 Candles on a 210 kg Cake** - To celebrate the 70th Indian Independence Day, Dr. Pillai attempted to light 70,000 candles on a 210 kg cake, which was recorded in World Records India.

Attempted - **Documentary on Dhamek Stupa of Sarnath in 17 Languages** - Dr. Pillai attempted to create a documentary on the Dhamek Stupa of Sarnath, dubbing it in 17 different languages. The result of this attempt is currently awaiting confirmation from the Guinness World Records.

Dr. Pillai is skilled in teaching the Bhagavad Gita, a Hindu scripture, and is popular among young people. He has helped many young people improve their lives through his motivational teachings.

In addition to teaching, he has composed and sung numerous Sanskrit Bhajans and patriotic songs.

He has also written and directed several short films and documentaries for awareness campaigns, and has volunteered with the police in both UP and Kerala to spread awareness about various issues through videos and photography.

Incredibly, he has produced and directed over 100 documentaries about the city of Varanasi, all on his own.

He has also helped and guided more than 25 boys and girls to achieve world records through creative and innovative methods. He is a multifaceted person who uses his intellect and the blessings given to him by God to excel in various areas. He is both a teacher and a student, always learning and teaching, and is able to master any subject he comes across.

He is a selfless social activist and motivational speaker who has overcome struggles and failures to become a successful and enthusiastic individual with a rich life experience.

In addition to his work with the Bhagavad Gita, he is also an efficient Tarot card reader, Astro-Vastu consultant, and a talented singer and composer. He has sung the entire Ram Charita Manas and Bhagavad Gita in his own compositions, and has sung the phrase "Lokah Samastha Sukhino Bhavantu" in 50 different languages. He is currently working on a detailed and scientific study of Vedas, Upanishads, Puranas, and the Bhagavad Gita. He has also composed and sung the Hanuman Chalisa and Gayatri Mantra in 108 and 1008 different compositions, respectively.

Awards - Four Times Guinness World Records, Winner of Mahatma Gandhi Vishwa Shanti Puraskar, Mahatma Gandhi Global Peace Ambassador, Kashi Ratna Award, Dr. APJ Abdul Kalam Motivational Person of the Year 2017, Mother Teresa Award, Indira Gandhi Priyadarshini Award, Bharat Vikas Ratna Award, Udyog Ratna Award, Vigyan Prasar Award, Poorvanchal Ratn Samman.

Preface

We all have moments of self-doubt and insecurity. But what if we could learn to accept ourselves and build our confidence? That is the goal of Building Confidence Through Self-Love: A Guide to Achieving Self-Acceptance. This book is designed to help readers understand the power of self-love and how to use it to build confidence and achieve self-acceptance.

This book is a comprehensive guide to understanding the importance of self-love and how to use it to build confidence. It covers topics such as understanding the power of self-love, developing self-awareness, and learning to accept yourself. It also provides practical advice on how to use self-love to build confidence and achieve self-acceptance.

The book is written in an accessible and engaging style, making it easy to understand and apply the concepts to your own life. It is filled with inspiring stories and practical tips to help you on your journey to self-acceptance.

Building Confidence Through Self-Love: A Guide to Achieving Self-Acceptance is an invaluable resource for anyone looking to build their confidence and learn to accept themselves. It is a must-read for anyone who wants to learn how to use self-love to build their confidence and achieve self-acceptance. With this book, you will gain the knowledge and tools you need to take control of your life and become the confident, self-accepting person you want to be.

• xiv •

I

Understanding Self-Love

Self-love is an essential aspect of building confidence and achieving self-acceptance. It is the foundation of a healthy and fulfilling life, as it enables individuals to value themselves and appreciate who they are, flaws and all.

Self-love is a holistic experience that encompasses different aspects of one's life. It's about accepting one's thoughts, feelings, and behaviors as well as appreciating one's physical appearance, abilities, and strengths.

Self-love is often mistaken for selfishness or arrogance, but it is not the same. Self-love is a healthy and balanced form of love that prioritizes one's well-being and happiness, while still respecting others and their feelings.

The lack of self-love can lead to negative consequences such as low self-esteem, anxiety, depression, and unhealthy relationships. On the other hand, people who cultivate self-love tend to have high self-esteem, better relationships, and a more positive outlook on life.

There are several key components of self-love, including self-compassion, self-awareness, and self-care.

Self-compassion involves treating oneself with kindness, empathy, and understanding, even during difficult times or when mistakes are made. This can help to reduce negative self-talk and increase positive self-affirmations.

Self-awareness is the process of understanding one's thoughts, feelings, and behaviors and how they influence one's life. By becoming more self-aware, individuals can gain insight into their patterns of thinking and behavior and work towards making positive changes.

Self-care is the act of taking care of one's physical, emotional, and mental health. This includes activities such as eating well, exercising regularly, getting enough sleep, and engaging in hobbies or interests that bring joy.

It is important to note that self-love is a lifelong journey and requires constant effort and practice. Negative self-talk and old habits can be difficult to break, but with time and dedication, self-love can become a natural and integral part of one's life.

In conclusion, understanding self-love is crucial to building confidence and achieving self-acceptance. It involves treating oneself with kindness and empathy, gaining self-awareness, and engaging in self-care. By prioritizing self-love, individuals can create a more fulfilling and happy life.

"*Self-love is the foundation of true confidence;
it is the key to unlocking your potential.*"

&

II

Exploring Self-Love Practices

Self-love practices are crucial for building confidence and achieving self-acceptance. These practices help individuals cultivate self-love and make it an integral part of their lives. In this chapter, we will explore some self-love practices that individuals can incorporate into their daily routine.

Positive self-talk: Positive self-talk is a powerful tool for cultivating self-love. It involves speaking kindly to oneself and replacing negative self-talk with positive affirmations. Some examples of positive affirmations include "I am worthy and deserving of love," "I am capable of achieving my goals," and "I am enough just as I am."

Gratitude journaling: Keeping a gratitude journal is a great way to focus on the positive aspects of one's life and cultivate self-love. Individuals can write down things they are grateful for each day, no matter how small they may seem. This practice helps to shift focus away from negative thoughts and towards the things in life that bring joy and happiness.

Self-care: Self-care is an important aspect of self-love and involves taking care of one's physical, emotional, and mental well-being. This can include activities such as exercise, healthy eating, getting enough sleep, and engaging in hobbies or interests that bring joy.

Mindfulness meditation: Mindfulness meditation involves being present in the moment and focusing on one's thoughts and feelings. This practice helps to increase self-awareness and reduce negative self-talk. Individuals can start with short meditation sessions, gradually increasing the time as they become more comfortable with the practice.

Surrounding oneself with positive people: Surrounding oneself with positive and supportive individuals can help to boost self-esteem and increase feelings of self-love. It's important to surround oneself with people who are encouraging and uplifting, rather than those who bring negativity into one's life.

Celebrating accomplishments: Celebrating accomplishments, no matter how small, is a great way to increase feelings of self-love. This can involve taking time to acknowledge and appreciate one's achievements and giving oneself credit for hard work and dedication.

Treating oneself with kindness and compassion: Treating oneself with kindness and compassion is a crucial aspect of self-love. This involves being gentle with oneself, even during difficult times, and recognizing that everyone makes mistakes.

In conclusion, self-love practices are an important tool for building confidence and achieving self-acceptance. They involve positive self-talk, gratitude journaling, self-care, mindfulness meditation, surrounding oneself with positive people, celebrating accomplishments, and treating oneself with kindness and compassion. By incorporating these practices into one's daily routine, individuals can cultivate self-love and make it an integral part of their lives.

"The journey to self-acceptance begins with self-love; it is the first step to building confidence."

ॐ

III

Developing a Self-Love Mindset

Developing a self-love mindset is an important step in building confidence and achieving self-acceptance. A self-love mindset involves a deep understanding and acceptance of oneself, along with a belief in one's own worth and value. In this chapter, we will explore some key elements of a self-love mindset and how individuals can develop it.

Understanding one's worth: Understanding one's worth and value as an individual is a critical aspect of a self-love mindset. This involves recognizing that one's worth is not based on external factors such as appearance, achievements, or material possessions. Instead, one's worth is inherent and cannot be taken away.

Accepting oneself: Accepting oneself, including one's strengths and weaknesses, is a crucial aspect of a self-love mindset. This involves being kind and compassionate towards oneself, rather than engaging in negative self-talk or criticism.

Recognizing negative self-talk: Negative self-talk is a common barrier to developing a self-love mindset. Recognizing this type of self-talk and working to replace it with positive affirmations is an important step in building a self-love mindset.

Challenging limiting beliefs: Limiting beliefs, such as "I'm not good enough," "I'll never be successful," or "I don't deserve love," can hold individuals back from developing a self-love mindset. Challenging these limiting beliefs and replacing them with more positive and empowering beliefs is an important step in building a self-love mindset.

Fostering self-compassion: Self-compassion is an important aspect of a self-love mindset. It involves being kind and understanding towards oneself, especially during difficult times. This can involve practices such as self-care, mindfulness meditation, and engaging in activities that bring joy and happiness.

Surrounding oneself with positive influences: Surrounding oneself with positive and supportive individuals can help to boost self-esteem and increase feelings of self-love. It's important to surround oneself with people who are encouraging and uplifting, rather than those who bring negativity into one's life.

Practicing self-love regularly: Incorporating self-love practices into one's daily routine is a crucial step in developing a self-love mindset. This can involve positive self-talk, gratitude journaling, self-care, mindfulness meditation, and celebrating accomplishments.

In conclusion, developing a self-love mindset is an important step in building confidence and achieving self-acceptance. It involves understanding one's worth, accepting oneself, recognizing negative self-talk, challenging limiting beliefs, fostering self-compassion, surrounding oneself with positive influences, and practicing self-love regularly. By incorporating these elements into one's life, individuals can develop a strong self-love mindset and build confidence in themselves and their abilities.

"You are the only one who can give yourself
the love and acceptance you need to build
confidence."

∞

IV
Reframing Negative Thoughts

Negative thoughts and self-doubt can be major obstacles on the journey to self-love and self-acceptance. These negative thoughts can lead to feelings of low self-worth, insecurity, and a lack of confidence. In this chapter, we will explore the importance of reframing negative thoughts and how to do it.

Recognize negative thoughts: The first step in reframing negative thoughts is to recognize them. This can be done by becoming aware of your thoughts and patterns of self-talk. Pay attention to the thoughts that are holding you back and preventing you from feeling confident and loved.

Challenge negative thoughts: Once you have identified your negative thoughts, the next step is to challenge them. Ask yourself if the thought is based on fact or if it is just a perception. Ask yourself if the thought is helpful or if it is just causing stress and anxiety.

Replace negative thoughts with positive ones: Once you have challenged your negative thoughts, replace them with positive, empowering thoughts. Focus on your strengths, accomplishments, and positive qualities. Repeat these positive thoughts to yourself often and believe in them.

Practice gratitude: Practicing gratitude is a great way to reframe negative thoughts and focus on the positive aspects of your life. Take time each day to reflect on the things you are grateful for and focus on these things instead of your negative thoughts.

Surround yourself with positive people: Surrounding yourself with positive, supportive people can help you reframe negative thoughts and build confidence. Seek out relationships with people who are encouraging, understanding, and non-judgmental.

Find a creative outlet: Find a creative outlet that allows you to express yourself and reframe negative thoughts. This could be writing, painting, dancing, or any other form of self-expression. When you engage in creative activities, you can release negative emotions and focus on the positive aspects of your life.

Seek professional help: If negative thoughts are causing significant distress, seek the help of a mental health professional. A professional can help you reframe negative thoughts, develop coping strategies, and improve your overall well-being.

In conclusion, negative thoughts and self-doubt can be major obstacles on the journey to self-love and self-acceptance. Reframing negative thoughts is an important aspect of building confidence and improving self-esteem. Recognize negative thoughts, challenge them, replace them with positive ones, practice gratitude, surround yourself with positive people, find a creative outlet, and seek professional help when necessary. By reframing negative thoughts, you can develop a more positive and confident mindset and achieve self-love and self-acceptance.

"The path to self-acceptance starts with self-love; it is the key to unlocking your true potential and achieving your goals."

ॐ

V
Overcoming Self-Doubt

Self-doubt can be a major barrier to building confidence and achieving self-acceptance. It can lead individuals to second-guess their abilities, decisions, and worth, causing them to feel insecure and uncertain. In this chapter, we will explore some strategies for overcoming self-doubt and building confidence.

Identifying self-doubt: The first step in overcoming self-doubt is to identify when it occurs. This may involve paying attention to thoughts and feelings, as well as noting physical sensations that accompany self-doubt.

Challenging negative thoughts: Negative thoughts can be a major contributor to self-doubt. Challenging these thoughts by questioning their validity and replacing them with more positive and empowering thoughts is an important step in overcoming self-doubt.

Practicing self-compassion: Self-compassion can be a powerful tool in overcoming self-doubt. It involves treating oneself with kindness and understanding, rather than engaging in negative self-talk or criticism. This can help to boost self-esteem and increase feelings of self-worth.

Fostering positive self-talk: Positive self-talk is a critical component of overcoming self-doubt. Engaging in positive self-talk, such as affirmations and self-encouragement, can help to boost confidence and counteract negative thoughts.

Building self-awareness: Building self-awareness and understanding one's own thoughts and emotions can be a valuable tool in overcoming self-doubt. This involves paying attention to one's own thought patterns and recognizing when negative thoughts are arising.

Celebrating successes: Celebrating successes, no matter how small, is an important step in overcoming self-doubt. This helps to build self-confidence and counteract negative self-talk.

Seeking support: Seeking support from friends, family, or a mental health professional can be a valuable tool in overcoming self-doubt. Talking about one's thoughts and feelings can help to increase self-awareness and reduce self-doubt.

In conclusion, overcoming self-doubt is a critical step in building confidence and achieving self-acceptance. This can involve identifying self-doubt, challenging negative thoughts, practicing self-compassion, fostering positive self-talk, building self-awareness, celebrating successes, and seeking support. By incorporating these strategies into one's life, individuals can overcome self-doubt and build confidence in themselves and their abilities.

"Self-love is the key to unlocking your inner
strength and courage."

VI
Embracing Your Strengths

Embracing one's strengths is an essential component of building confidence and achieving self-acceptance. By focusing on what we are good at and what we bring to the table, we can increase feelings of self-worth and reduce self-doubt. In this chapter, we will explore ways to identify and embrace our strengths.

Identifying strengths: The first step in embracing our strengths is to identify what they are. This may involve reflecting on our past experiences and accomplishments, asking friends and family for their perspective, and taking personality and strengths assessments.

Acknowledging and accepting strengths: Once our strengths have been identified, it is important to acknowledge and accept them. This means embracing our strengths, even if they may not be viewed as "perfect" by others.

Leveraging strengths: Leveraging our strengths is an important step in building confidence and achieving self-acceptance. This involves using our strengths in our personal and professional lives, and seeking out opportunities to utilize them.

Cultivating a growth mindset: Cultivating a growth mindset, or a belief that our abilities can be developed through effort and learning, can help us to embrace our strengths. This involves viewing challenges as opportunities for growth and development.

Fostering gratitude: Fostering gratitude for our strengths can help us to embrace them and increase feelings of self-worth. This involves regularly reflecting on and appreciating our strengths, and recognizing the impact they have on our lives and the lives of others.

Celebrating successes: Celebrating our successes, no matter how small, is an important step in embracing our strengths. This helps to build self-confidence and counteract negative self-talk.

Surrounding ourselves with positivity: Surrounding ourselves with positive, supportive people can help us to embrace our strengths and build confidence. This involves seeking out relationships with individuals who encourage and uplift us, and avoiding those who bring negativity into our lives.

In conclusion, embracing our strengths is an important

component of building confidence and achieving self-acceptance. This can involve identifying our strengths, acknowledging and accepting them, leveraging them, cultivating a growth mindset, fostering gratitude, celebrating successes, and surrounding ourselves with positivity. By embracing our strengths, we can increase feelings of self-worth and reduce self-doubt, and build a strong foundation for confidence and self-acceptance.

"The power of self-love is the power to create a
life of confidence and joy."

ॐ

VII

Being Kind to Yourself

Self-love is about valuing and accepting yourself for who you are, and being kind to yourself is a crucial aspect of this process. In this chapter, we will delve into why it is important to be kind to yourself and provide tips for doing so.

The Importance of Being Kind to Yourself

Being kind to yourself is not just a feel-good practice, it has real and tangible benefits. When you are kind to yourself, you are creating a positive inner dialogue that can have a profound impact on your mental and emotional wellbeing. Research has shown that treating ourselves with kindness and compassion can help to reduce anxiety and depression, increase resilience, and boost self-esteem.

Moreover, being kind to yourself is essential for building

self-confidence. When you are kind to yourself, you are sending a message to your subconscious mind that you are worthy of love, respect, and acceptance. This, in turn, will help you to build a stronger sense of self-worth and develop a more positive self-image.

Tips for Being Kind to Yourself

Here are some tips for being kind to yourself:

Practice self-compassion: Self-compassion is the act of treating yourself with the same kindness and understanding that you would offer to a good friend. It involves acknowledging your feelings, being non-judgmental, and offering yourself words of encouragement and support.

Be mindful of your self-talk: Your self-talk can have a significant impact on your self-esteem and confidence. Be mindful of the things you say to yourself, and make an effort to replace negative self-talk with positive affirmations.

Engage in self-care activities: Taking care of your physical and emotional needs is a vital aspect of self-love. Engage in activities that bring you joy and relaxation, such as taking a bath, practicing yoga, or reading a book.

Give yourself permission to make mistakes: No one is perfect, and it's essential to understand that it's okay to make mistakes. When you do, remind yourself that everyone makes mistakes, and that they don't define you as a person.

Celebrate your accomplishments: Take the time to acknowledge and celebrate your accomplishments, no matter how small they may be. Celebrating your successes helps to build self-confidence and reinforces the message that you are capable and deserving of success.

Being kind to yourself is an essential aspect of building self-confidence and achieving self-acceptance. It involves treating yourself with compassion, engaging in self-care activities, and embracing your imperfections. By making a conscious effort to be kind to yourself, you can cultivate a positive self-image, reduce stress, and boost your overall wellbeing.

"Self-love is the key to unlocking your true
potential and achieving your goals."

৪৩

VIII
Appreciating Your Achievements

In this chapter, we will focus on the importance of appreciating your achievements and provide tips for doing so. Self-love is about recognizing and accepting all aspects of yourself, including your achievements, and this is a crucial component of building confidence and self-acceptance.

The Importance of Appreciating Your Achievements

Appreciating your achievements is essential for building self-confidence and a positive self-image. It allows you to acknowledge and celebrate your hard work and accomplishments, which reinforces the message that you are capable and deserving of success. This, in turn, can help to boost your self-esteem and increase your motivation to continue striving towards your goals.

Moreover, appreciating your achievements can help to combat impostor syndrome, a phenomenon in which individuals feel like frauds despite their accomplishments. By recognizing and celebrating your achievements, you are sending a message to your subconscious mind that you are worthy and deserving of success, which can help to overcome feelings of inadequacy and self-doubt.

Tips for Appreciating Your Achievements

Here are some tips for appreciating your achievements:

Keep a gratitude journal: Write down your achievements, big or small, in a gratitude journal. Reflecting on your accomplishments can help to cultivate feelings of gratitude and boost your self-confidence.

Celebrate your successes: Take the time to celebrate your achievements, no matter how small they may be. This can be as simple as treating yourself to a special meal or purchasing a small item that you have been eyeing.

Share your accomplishments with others: Sharing your achievements with others can help to reinforce the message that you are capable and deserving of success. This can also help to build a support network of people who are cheering you on and celebrating your accomplishments.

Reframe negative self-talk: When you are feeling down or discouraged, it can be easy to focus on your failures and neglect to acknowledge your achievements. Make an effort to reframe negative self-talk by focusing on your successes and the progress that you have made.

Create a visual representation of your achievements: Create a visual representation of your achievements, such as a vision board or a scrapbook. Having a physical representation of your accomplishments can help to reinforce the message that you are capable and deserving of success.

Appreciating your achievements is an essential aspect of building self-confidence and self-acceptance. It allows you to acknowledge and celebrate your hard work and accomplishments, which reinforces the message that you are capable and deserving of success. By making a conscious effort to appreciate your achievements, you can boost your self-esteem, increase your motivation, and combat impostor syndrome. So, take the time to celebrate your successes and give yourself the recognition that you deserve.

"The path to self-acceptance starts with self-love; it is the foundation of true confidence."

‮ଓ‬

IX

Celebrating Your Uniqueness

In this chapter, we will explore the importance of celebrating your uniqueness and provide tips for doing so. Self-love is about embracing and accepting all aspects of yourself, including your unique qualities and quirks, and this is a crucial component of building confidence and self-acceptance.

The Importance of Celebrating Your Uniqueness

Celebrating your uniqueness is essential for building self-confidence and a positive self-image. When you embrace and celebrate your unique qualities and quirks, you are sending a message to yourself that you are worthy and deserving of love and acceptance, just as you are. This, in turn, can help to boost your self-esteem and increase your motivation to continue striving towards your goals.

Moreover, celebrating your uniqueness can help to combat feelings of inadequacy and comparison. It is easy to fall into the trap of comparing ourselves to others and feeling like we don't measure up. However, by embracing and celebrating your unique qualities and quirks, you are embracing your individuality and rejecting the notion that you need to conform to societal norms and expectations.

Tips for Celebrating Your Uniqueness

Here are some tips for celebrating your uniqueness:

Embrace your quirks and differences: Embrace your quirks and differences, even if they are not conventional or socially accepted. These unique qualities are what make you, you, and are what set you apart from everyone else.

Write a letter to yourself: Write a letter to yourself highlighting your unique qualities and quirks. Reflect on what makes you special and unique, and express gratitude for these qualities.

Surround yourself with people who accept and love you for who you are: Surround yourself with people who celebrate and embrace your uniqueness, rather than try to change you. These people will be a source of support and encouragement as you navigate your journey towards self-acceptance.

Embrace your hobbies and interests: Embrace your hobbies and interests, even if they are not conventional or popular. Pursuing these interests can help to reinforce the message that you are worthy and deserving of love and acceptance, just as you are.

Practice self-compassion: Practice self-compassion by acknowledging and accepting your flaws and imperfections. Rather than being critical and harsh towards yourself, embrace your imperfections as a part of what makes you, you.

Celebrating your uniqueness is an essential aspect of building self-confidence and self-acceptance. When you embrace and celebrate your unique qualities and quirks, you are sending a message to yourself that you are worthy and deserving of love and acceptance, just as you are. By making a conscious effort to celebrate your uniqueness, you can boost your self-esteem, increase your motivation, and combat feelings of inadequacy and comparison. So, embrace your individuality and reject the notion that you need to conform to societal norms and expectations. Celebrate your uniqueness and love yourself for who you are.

"The power of self-love is the power to create a
life of courage and resilience."

જી

X

Learning to Accept and Love Yourself

In this chapter, we will explore the concept of self-acceptance and provide tips for learning to accept and love yourself. Self-love is about embracing and accepting all aspects of yourself, and this includes your flaws and imperfections. By learning to accept and love yourself, you will lay the foundation for building self-confidence and a positive self-image.

The Importance of Self-Acceptance

Self-acceptance is the foundation of self-love. When you are able to accept and love yourself, flaws and all, you are sending a message to yourself that you are worthy and deserving of love and respect, just as you are. This, in turn, can help to boost your self-esteem and increase your motivation to continue striving towards your goals.

Moreover, self-acceptance can help to combat feelings of inadequacy and comparison. When you are able to accept and love yourself, you are less likely to compare yourself to others and feel like you don't measure up. Instead, you will focus on your own journey and progress, rather than comparing yourself to others.

Tips for Learning to Accept and Love Yourself

Here are some tips for learning to accept and love yourself:

Practice self-compassion: Practice self-compassion by acknowledging and accepting your flaws and imperfections. Rather than being critical and harsh towards yourself, embrace your imperfections as a part of what makes you, you.

Embrace your hobbies and interests: Embrace your hobbies and interests, even if they are not conventional or popular. Pursuing these interests can help to reinforce the message that you are worthy and deserving of love and acceptance, just as you are.

Surround yourself with positive people: Surround yourself with people who are positive and supportive, rather than those who are critical and negative. These people will be a source of support and encouragement as you navigate your journey towards self-acceptance.

Practice gratitude: Practice gratitude by focusing on the things in your life that you are thankful for, rather than dwelling on your flaws and imperfections. This can help to shift your focus from what you lack to what you have, and increase your overall sense of happiness and well-being.

Embrace your unique qualities and quirks: Embrace your unique qualities and quirks, even if they are not conventional or socially accepted. These unique qualities are what make you, you, and are what set you apart from everyone else.

Write a letter to yourself: Write a letter to yourself highlighting your strengths and achievements. Reflect on what makes you special and unique, and express gratitude for these qualities.

Learning to accept and love yourself is a crucial aspect of building self-confidence and self-acceptance. When you are able to accept and love yourself, flaws and all, you are sending a message to yourself that you are worthy and deserving of love and respect, just as you are. By making a conscious effort to practice self-compassion, embrace your unique qualities, surround yourself with positive people, and focus on gratitude, you can lay the foundation for building self-confidence and a positive self-image. So, embrace yourself, flaws and all, and love yourself for who you are.

"Self-love is the key to unlocking your inner courage and strength to face any challenge."

⚮

XI

Dealing with Criticism

In this chapter, we will discuss the challenges of dealing with criticism and provide tips for managing and overcoming it. Criticism can be difficult to handle, especially if it feels like it is directed at you personally. However, criticism can be a valuable tool for self-reflection and growth, if approached in the right way.

The Importance of Dealing with Criticism

Dealing with criticism is an important part of building self-confidence and self-acceptance. Criticism can be hurtful, but it can also be an opportunity to learn and grow. By managing and overcoming criticism, you can build resilience and self-confidence, and improve your overall well-being.

Moreover, criticism can help you to identify areas for

improvement and growth. By taking constructive criticism to heart, and using it as a tool for growth, you can make meaningful changes and improve your life.

Tips for Dealing with Criticism

Here are some tips for dealing with criticism:

Separate the criticism from the person: It can be tempting to take criticism personally, but it's important to remember that criticism is not a reflection of your character. Instead, try to view the criticism objectively and focus on the message being conveyed.

Identify the source of the criticism: Criticism can come from a variety of sources, including friends, family, coworkers, and even strangers. Understanding the source of the criticism can help you to better comprehend the motivation behind it, and respond in an appropriate manner.

Distinguish between constructive and destructive criticism: Not all criticism is beneficial. Some criticism is constructive, and is intended to help you develop and progress. Other criticism is destructive, and is meant to be hurtful. It is important to be able to recognize the difference between the two, and respond accordingly.

Take time to reflect: After receiving criticism, it is important to take some time to reflect on it. Consider the criticism objectively, and think about how it can help you to improve. If the criticism is valid, use it as an opportunity to learn and grow. If it is not, then simply let it go.

"The journey to self-acceptance begins with self-love; it is the first step to unlocking your true potential."

୧

XII

Finding Self-Acceptance Through Forgiveness

Forgiveness is an essential component of self-acceptance and can bring peace to your heart, mind, and soul. The act of forgiving is not just about letting go of anger, resentment, and pain, but it's about freeing yourself from negative emotions and embracing a new outlook on life.

Self-forgiveness is a crucial step in the journey towards self-acceptance. Most of us have moments in our lives when we feel guilty, ashamed, or embarrassed about something we've done or said. Holding onto these negative emotions can lead to self-doubt, low self-esteem, and a negative self-image. It's essential to understand that forgiving yourself is not about condoning bad behavior, but rather it's about acknowledging that you made a mistake and learning from it.

Forgiving others is also an essential aspect of self-acceptance. We all have people in our lives who have hurt us in one way or another. Holding onto grudges and resentment towards these people can lead to negative thoughts and emotions, which can interfere with our ability to be happy and content. Forgiveness doesn't mean forgetting what happened or condoning the behavior. It's about releasing negative emotions and focusing on the positive aspects of your life.

Here are some steps to help you forgive yourself and others:

Acknowledge your feelings: The first step in the forgiveness process is to acknowledge the feelings of anger, pain, and resentment that you may be holding onto. Allow yourself to feel these emotions without judgment, and be patient with yourself as you work through them.

Practice self-compassion: Treat yourself with kindness and understanding. Remind yourself that everyone makes mistakes, and that it's a normal part of being human.

Reframe your thoughts: Reframe negative thoughts about yourself and others into positive ones. Focus on what you can learn from the situation and how it can make you stronger.

Write it down: Writing down your thoughts and feelings can be an effective way to release negative emotions and help you process them. Consider writing a letter to yourself or to the person you're forgiving, expressing your thoughts and feelings.

Let it go: Once you've worked through your emotions, it's time to let them go. This can be done through visualization, meditation, or simply telling yourself that you're ready to release the negative feelings.

Forgiving yourself and others can be a challenging process, but the benefits are well worth it. When you practice forgiveness, you open yourself up to self-acceptance and a more positive outlook on life. You'll find that you have more energy, motivation, and peace of mind, and you'll be better equipped to handle the challenges that life throws your way.

In conclusion, self-acceptance and forgiveness are closely linked. Forgiving yourself and others allows you to let go of negative emotions and focus on the positive aspects of your life. Embracing self-forgiveness and self-compassion can help you build confidence and lead a life filled with peace, happiness, and contentment.

"You are the only one who can give yourself
the love and acceptance you need to build a
life of confidence and joy."

౫

XIII

Taking Care of Your Body

Your body is a temple, and taking care of it is an important aspect of self-love and self-acceptance. When you nurture your physical health, you not only improve your appearance, but you also enhance your mental, emotional, and spiritual well-being. In this chapter, we'll explore how taking care of your body can help you build confidence and achieve self-acceptance.

Exercise regularly: Exercise is essential for physical and mental well-being. Regular exercise can help improve your posture, increase your energy levels, and enhance your mood. When you exercise, your body releases endorphins, which are natural mood boosters. Aim for at least 30 minutes of moderate exercise every day, whether it's running, yoga, or walking.

Eat a healthy diet: A balanced diet is essential for maintaining good health. Include a variety of fruits, vegetables, whole grains, and lean protein in your diet. Avoid processed foods, sugar, and excessive amounts of salt and caffeine. Eating a healthy diet can help you maintain a healthy weight, increase your energy levels, and reduce the risk of chronic diseases.

Hydrate: Drinking plenty of water is crucial for your health. Water helps regulate your body temperature, removes waste, and maintains healthy skin. Aim to drink at least 8 glasses of water a day.

Get enough sleep: Sleep is essential for physical and mental recovery. Aim for 7-9 hours of sleep each night. Create a bedtime routine that helps you relax, such as reading a book, taking a warm bath, or meditating.

Practice self-care: Taking care of your body also involves taking care of your skin, hair, and nails. Regular grooming and self-care rituals, such as getting a massage or taking a bubble bath, can help you feel refreshed and rejuvenated.

Avoid harmful habits: Habits such as smoking, excessive alcohol consumption, and drug use can have a negative impact on your health and well-being. If you have any harmful habits, consider seeking support to help you quit.

Celebrate your body: Celebrate your body and all that it can do. Practice gratitude for your body by acknowledging its strengths and abilities. Engage in activities that make you feel good about your body, such as dancing, hiking, or playing sports.

In conclusion, taking care of your body is an important aspect of self-love and self-acceptance. Regular exercise, a healthy diet, and self-care rituals can help you feel confident, strong, and healthy. When you nurture your physical health, you'll find that you have more energy, motivation, and peace of mind, and you'll be better equipped to handle the challenges that life throws your way. Remember, your body is a temple, and taking care of it is an act of self-love and self-acceptance.

"Self-love is the foundation of true confidence;
it is the key to unlocking your inner strength
and courage."

෨

XIV

Creating Healthy Boundaries

Healthy boundaries are essential for building self-confidence and achieving self-acceptance. Boundaries help you define who you are, what you want, and what you're willing to accept from others. When you have clear boundaries, you are better equipped to protect yourself from being taken advantage of, being mistreated, or becoming overburdened with other people's problems. In this chapter, we'll explore how creating healthy boundaries can help you build confidence and achieve self-acceptance.

Identify your boundaries: The first step in creating healthy boundaries is to identify what you want and don't want in your life. This includes the types of behavior, interactions, and relationships that you are willing to accept. Write down your boundaries and what they mean to you.

Communicate your boundaries: Once you have identified

your boundaries, it's important to communicate them clearly to others. This can be done in a calm, assertive manner, without being aggressive or confrontational. When communicating your boundaries, use "I" statements, such as "I feel uncomfortable when..." or "I need..." to avoid blaming or accusing others.

Respect others' boundaries: It's important to respect the boundaries of others, just as you would want them to respect yours. If someone communicates their boundaries to you, listen to them, and try to understand their perspective. Don't try to push their boundaries or ignore their wishes.

Enforce your boundaries: Once you've communicated your boundaries, it's important to enforce them. If someone is violating your boundaries, calmly and assertively remind them of your boundaries and the consequences if they continue to violate them. If necessary, remove yourself from the situation or relationship if your boundaries are repeatedly being violated.

Practice self-care: Taking care of yourself is an important aspect of creating healthy boundaries. This includes setting aside time for yourself, engaging in activities that you enjoy, and protecting your physical, mental, and emotional health. When you prioritize your self-care, you are better equipped to maintain your boundaries and protect yourself from being taken advantage of.

Seek support: Creating healthy boundaries can be challenging, especially if you have a history of not setting boundaries or of being in unhealthy relationships. If you need support, consider seeking help from a therapist or counselor.

In conclusion, creating healthy boundaries is an important aspect of building self-confidence and achieving self-acceptance. When you have clear boundaries, you are better equipped to protect yourself from being taken advantage of, being mistreated, or becoming overburdened with other people's problems. Remember, your boundaries are your responsibility, and you have the right to define and enforce them in a way that works for you. By practicing self-care and seeking support when necessary, you can create and maintain healthy boundaries and build confidence in yourself and your decisions.

"The power of self-love is the power to create a
life of resilience and courage."

ରଙ

XV

Connecting with Others on the Journey to Self-Love

Self-love and self-acceptance are not just individual pursuits, but also social ones. Building a supportive network of people who understand and respect your journey can be instrumental in achieving self-love and confidence. In this chapter, we will explore the importance of connecting with others on the journey to self-love and self-acceptance.

Surround yourself with positive people: Surrounding yourself with positive, supportive people is important for building self-confidence and achieving self-acceptance. This includes family members, friends, and coworkers who are encouraging, understanding, and non-judgmental. Seek out relationships with people who are genuinely interested in your growth and well-being.

Join a support group: Joining a support group can be a great way to connect with others who are on a similar journey. Support groups can provide a safe and supportive environment to discuss your experiences, receive feedback, and gain perspective. They can also provide you with a sense of community and a sense of belonging.

Volunteer: Volunteering can help you connect with others while also making a positive impact on your community. When you volunteer, you can connect with others who share your values and interests, and you can also learn new skills and gain new experiences.

Participate in online communities: There are many online communities where people can connect with others who are on a similar journey. This includes social media groups, forums, and discussion boards. Participating in online communities can provide a supportive and non-judgmental environment where you can discuss your experiences and receive feedback.

Seek out mentors: Seek out people who have already achieved the level of self-love and self-acceptance that you strive for. These people can serve as mentors, providing you with guidance, support, and inspiration. When you have a mentor, you can learn from their experiences, gain new perspectives, and receive feedback on your own journey.

Practice gratitude: Practice gratitude by focusing on the positive aspects of your relationships and experiences. This will help you cultivate a positive attitude and increase your appreciation for the people and experiences in your life.

In conclusion, connecting with others is an important aspect of building self-confidence and achieving self-acceptance. Surrounding yourself with positive, supportive people, participating in support groups, volunteering, participating in online communities, seeking out mentors, and practicing gratitude can help you build a supportive network of people who understand and respect your journey. Remember, you are not alone on this journey, and connecting with others can provide you with the support and encouragement you need to achieve self-love and self-acceptance.

"The journey to self-acceptance begins with self-love; it is the foundation upon which we can build a life of contentment and fulfillment."

෮

OTHER BOOKS OF THE AUTHOR

1. The Moments When I Met God
2. Kashiyile Theertha Pathangal
3. Guru Gyan Vani
4. Abhiprerak Gita
5. Assi Se Jain Ghat Tak
6. Hopelessness of Arjuna
7. The Soul and It's True Nature
8. Sense of Action (Karma)
9. Action Through Wisdom
10. Action Through Wisdom
11. Theory And Practical of Every Action
12. Logical Understanding of The Supreme
13. The Imperishable Supreme
14. Yatra Nishadraj Se Hanuman Ghat Tak
15. Yatra Karnatak Ghat Se Raja Ghat Tak
16. Yatra Pandey Ghat Se Prayagraj Ghat Tak
17. Yatra Ranjendra Prasad Ghat Se Dattatreya Ghat Tak
18. Yaatrasindhiya Ghat Se Gwaliar Ghat Tak
19. Yatra Mangala Gauri Ghat Se Hanuman Gadhi Ghat Tak
20. Yatra Gaay Ghat Se Nishad Ghat Tak
21. Maa Ganga, Ghaten Evm Utsav
22. Ganga Arti Dev Deepavali Evam Any Utsav
23. Potentials of Digitalized India
24. Vedic Consciousness
25. A Brief Introduction to Vedic Science
26. Kashi Ke Barah Jyotirling
27. Impact Of Motivation
28. Let's Have a Milky Way Journey
29. Color Therapy in A Nutshell

30. Rigveda In a Nutshell
31. Yajurveda In a Nutshell
32. Samveda In a Nutshell
33. Atharva Veda In a Nutshell
34. Ayushman Bhava - Ayurveda
35. Srimad Bhagavad Gita and Upanishad Connection
36. Srimad Bhagavad Gita - An Attempt to Summarize Each Chapter.
37. Facts And Impact of Nakshatra
38. Astro Gems - Navaratna
39. Ekadashi - A Concise Overview
40. A Concise View of Hanuman Chalisa
41. Inspirational Gita
42. Nakshatraranyam
43. Summary of 18 Mahapuranas
44. Synopsis of 18 Upa Puranas
45. Rigvediya Upanishads
46. Shukla Yajurvediya Upanishads
47. Krishna Yajurvediya Upanishads
48. Samavediya Upanishads
49. Atharvavediya Upanishads
50. The Seven Great Sages
51. From Rocket Scientist to President Dr. Apj Abdul Kalam
52. The Visionary's Voice - Quotes of Dr. Apj Abdul Kalam
53. The Wisdom tf Swami Vivekananda: Insights and Inspiration from A Legendary Spiritual Teacher
54. Ayurvedic Remedies from The Garden
55. Sages and Seers
56. Rising Strong – Motivational Stories of Women
57. Beyond Flames -Mystery Stories of Funeral Ghat Manikarnika
58. The Origins of Tulsi: A Look at The Mythological Roots of The Plant"

121. Innovative Start-ups - 25 Start-up Ideas To Spark Your Business Creativity
122. Export Management: Strategies for Global Success
123. Exporting From India - A Step by Step Guide
124. Finance Fundamentals: Mastering Financial Management for Business Success
125. Global Growth Strategies for International Business Development
126. Marketing Mastery: Unlocking the Secrets of Modern Marketing
127. Operations Mastery: Managing the Flow of Value in Business
128. Strategic Business Management: Navigating the Modern Business Landscape
129. Human Resource Management Strategies for Building and Managing a High-Performance Team
130. The Indian Landscapes and Nature: An Exploration of India's Natural Beauty and Diversity
131. The Indian Street Performances: A Cultural Exploration of India's Street Performances
132. Affirming Your Self-Worth: Strategies for Achieving Emotional Wellbeing
133. Cultivating Self-Discipline: Secrets Methods for Achieving Your Goals
134. Embracing Change: Strategies for Adapting to Life's Challenges
135. Embracing Your Uniqueness: Secret Strategies for Living an Authentic Life
136. Finding Motivation in Despondency: Coping with Difficult Times
137. Embracing Change
138. Learning To Love Yourself
139. Managing Time for Yourself

Inner Peace

180. Finding Your Purpose: A Guide to Living an Authentic Life

181. Learning to Overcome Fear: A Guide to Achieving Your Goals

182. Mind Over Matter: Strategies for achieving Coherence and Concentration

183. Living with Intention: Strategies for Achieving Your Goals

184. Mastering Self-Compassion: A Guide to Nurturing Your Mind and Body

185. Mastering Self-Discipline: Strategies for Achieving Your Goals

186. Overcoming Negative Thinking: Strategies for Achieving Your Goals

187. Reclaiming Your Power: Strategies for Achieving Empowerment

188. Releasing Stress and Anxiety: A Guide to Achieving Balance

189. Setting Healthy Boundaries: Strategies for Protecting Yourself

190. Taking Control of Your Life: Strategies for Creating a Meaningful Future

191. Taking Responsibility for Your Life: Strategies for Achieving Self-Mastery

192. The Power of Positive Attitude: Strategies for Achieving Your Goals

193. Understanding Your Emotional Intelligence: Strategies for Living with Ease

CONTACT

DR. JAGADEESH PILLAI

MBA & PhD in Vedic Science

Four Times Guinness World Record Holder

Winner of Mahatma Gandhi Vishwa Shanti Puraskar and
Global Peace Ambassador

Gemology, Astro & Vastu Consultant - Spiritual Counselor

Consultant for designing World Record Ideas

Efficient Tarot Card Reader

9839093003

myrichindia@gmail.com

drjagadeeshpillai@facebook

drjagadeeshpillai@instagram
jagadeeshpillai@youtube

www. JAGADEESHPILLAI.com

|| LOKAHA SAMASTHAHA SUKHINO BHAVANTU ||

ॐ